Inexpensive Science Experiments

Grades 5-8

by
Pam Walker
and
Elaine Wood

Published by Instructional Fair
an imprint of
Frank Schaffer Publications

Instructional Fair

Authors: Pam Walker, Elaine Wood
Cover Artist: Jeff Van Kanegan
Interior Artist: Janet Armbrust
Photo Credits: © Image Club Graphics

Frank Schaffer Publicationsⁿ

Instructional Fair is an imprint of Frank Schaffer Publications.

Send all inquiries to:
Frank Schaffer Publications
3195 Wilson Drive NW
Grand Rapids, Michigan 49534

Inexpensive Science Experiments—grades 5–8

ISBN: 1-56822-957-7

4 5 6 7 8 9 10 11 PAT 10 09 08 07

Table of Contents

To the Teacher

Science activities and labs can be expensive, and not all science teachers have access to equipment and materials they need to perform many experiments. There are many good science activities that can be performed with inexpensive materials. This book provides some thought-provoking labs that can be done with everyday, low cost materials.

Inexpensive Science Experiments contains labs that encourage students to think. The materials used in these labs are inexpensive, and gathering them will be simple because they are easy to obtain. Gathering materials for these labs will be simple and quick.

Directions for the labs are clear and concise. Once the teacher provides the materials and directions, the learner can proceed at his/her own rate through the activity.

This book contains both life science and physical science activities. Each lab includes information for both the teacher and student. The teacher is provided with a Teacher Information page that includes the objectives of the lab, time required to perform the lab, teaching strategies, and an evaluation rubric. Any additional activity sheets or handouts the student will need to perform the activity are also provided for the teacher to photocopy. Students are provided with a Background Information page, Prelab Questions, a Procedure and Materials page, and a set of challenging Postlab Questions.

All activities included in this resource have been tested in the lab. The answer key provided at the back of the book provides you with anticipated results.

Bright Buttons

Objectives

Students will demonstrate how color affects natural selection.

Time Required

60 minutes

Teaching Strategies

Prior to the lab, have students read the Background Information and answer the Prelab Questions.

Divide the class into small groups of three or four.

Collect as many bright-colored and dark-colored buttons as you can. You may want to give extra credit points for students who bring buttons to class. Each lab group will need 20 bright and 20 dark buttons. Make certain the buttons used by a group are all similar in size.

Evaluation

Following is a suggested grading rubric:

Criteria	Points allowed	Points awarded
Prelab Questions correct	30	_____
Groups on task during the lab	20	_____
Activity sheet completed correctly	20	_____
Postlab Questions correct	30	_____
Total	100	_____

Bright Buttons

Nature can seem pretty harsh at times. Wouldn't it be nice if everything that was born lived in a nice home and had plenty to eat? You probably know that this is not true. There are many more organisms born than are able to survive. The environment does not provide enough food, water, and space for all offspring.

For example, fish lay hundreds of eggs. However, of all these eggs, fewer than ten live to be adults. In a nest of four baby birds, only one grows up to have babies of its own.

Characteristics of the individual babies help determine which ones will grow up and which ones will die young. One characteristic that can affect the survival of babies is color.

Baby animals that blend in with their surroundings are more likely to survive than those that do not blend in.

For example, many birds eat butterflies. The birds pick up butterflies that are easiest for them to see. In a group of young butterflies of the same kind, no two are just alike. Some are slightly larger than others. No two are exactly the same color.

Butterflies like to land on tree trunks to rest. In a forest of trees with dark trunks, darker butterflies blend in with the trunks better than lighter colored butterflies. Consequently, darker butterflies are camouflaged on dark trunks. When birds are looking for food, they can see lighter butterflies more easily than they can dark ones. That is why most of the butterflies they eat are light in color.

If you counted the number of light and dark butterflies living in an area where tree trunks are dark, you would find that there are more dark-colored ones living than light-colored ones. The dark-colored ones live long enough to produce offspring. In other words, the dark ones were the best survivors.

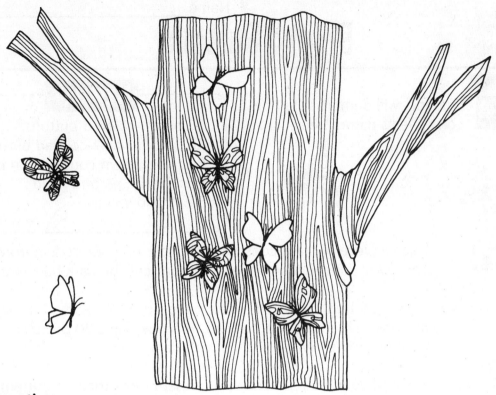

Prelab Questions

1. Would you expect all of the baby wolves born to a female wolf to live until adulthood? _____ Why or why not? _____

   _____

2. Give an example of an animal that is camouflaged by the environment. _____

3. Read the following scenarios and indicate which would be the most likely to survive.

   In a population of bats, some have a greater wingspan than others. Bats fly at night and catch insects. Which do you think would be most likely to survive: young bats with short wings or those with long wings? _____

   Why? _____

   _____

   In a population of deer living in the forest, most of the female deer produce fawns with mottled brown color. However, one deer's baby is an albino and is solid white. Which would be most likely to survive: a mottled brown fawn or a white fawn? _____ Why? _____

   _____

Bright Buttons

Objectives Students will demonstrate how color affects natural selection.

Materials

20 bright-colored buttons
20 black or dark-colored buttons
Black or brown construction paper
Watch with second hand
Small paper cup

Procedure

1. Place a piece of black construction paper on your desk in front of you. This black construction paper will represent the dark bark of a tree.

2. Obtain 20 bright-colored buttons and 20 dark-colored buttons. The buttons will represent butterflies. You now have 20 butterflies with brightly colored wings and 20 with dark wings.

3. You and your lab partners will represent birds that eat butterflies. Each partner will take turns following the same procedure.

   a. Place all 40 buttons in the cup and with your hand over the top of the cup, shake the cup. This will mix the buttons together.

   b. Carefully pour the buttons out on the dark construction paper. With your hand scatter the buttons so they are one layer deep.

   c. You now have 20 seconds to pick up as many buttons as possible. You may only pick up one button at a time.

   d. Record your name in Data Table 1 and how many buttons you were able to pick up. Also specify in Data Table 1 how many of the buttons were bright and how many were dark.

   e. Place all buttons back in the paper cup for the next partner to take his/her turn.

4. After all lab partners have completed their "bird feeding" turns, answer the conclusion questions.

Data Table 1. Results of button collection.

Partners' names	Column 1 Total number of buttons collected	Column 2 Number of bright buttons collected	Column 3 Number of dark buttons collected
1.			
2.			
3.			
4.			
Total			

Postlab Questions

1. Complete the Total part of the data table by adding the numbers in each column and recording them in the data table at the bottom of each of the three columns.

2. Find the percentage of bright-colored buttons collected in your group by dividing column 1 into column 2 and then moving the decimal place in your answer two places to the right. Show your work below.

3. Find the percentage of dark-colored buttons collected by your group by dividing column 1 into column 3 and moving the decimal place in your answer two places to the right. Show your work below.

4. Were your results in questions 2 and 3 as you expected, based on the laws of natural selection? _____ Explain your answer based on the dark tree bark and the dark- and bright-colored butterflies.

_____

_____

_____

_____

_____

Cool and Comfortable

Objectives Students will determine what types of fabric absorb the most water.

Time Required

30 minutes

Teaching Strategies

Prior to the lab, have students read the Background Information and answer the Prelab Questions.

Get your fabric samples from sewing scraps or from old, worn clothes. The color of fabric does not matter. You need enough samples of each type of fabric for every lab group. The size of the fabric samples is not specific, but each scrap must be cut to the same size.

In the front of the room, place the samples of cotton fabric in a bowl labeled A, the samples of wool fabric in a bowl labeled B, the samples of polyester fabric in a bowl labeled C, and the samples of silk fabric in a bowl labeled D.

You may want to have a few graduated cylinders or measuring cups on hand to quantify the differences in amount of water placed in each cup.

Evaluation Following is a suggested grading rubric:

Criteria	Points allowed	Points awarded
Prelab Questions correct	30	_____
Groups on task during the lab	20	_____
Data Table completed correctly	20	_____
Postlab Questions correct	30	_____
Total	100	_____

Cool and Comfortable

Manufacturers select the type of fabric to be used in clothing for a variety of reasons. One of these reasons is comfort. Some fabrics make more comfortable clothes for hot weather than other fabrics. Why is that? It seems that cloth that absorbs water, then releases the water by evaporation, feels good in the summer.

Evaporation is a cooling process. As water evaporates from a surface, it uses up some of the heat on that surface. Sweating is a cooling mechanism in people and many animals. Sweat is mostly water. When it evaporates from our skin, it cools us. Dogs also take advantage of the cooling effects of water as it evaporates. By salivating and panting, dogs release the heat from their bodies.

Prelab Questions

1. What natural mechanism do people have for cooling? _____

2. What mechanism do dogs have for cooling? _____

3. How does evaporation cool a surface? _____
_____

4. What kind of clothes are most comfortable in the summer: those that repel water, or those that absorb it and then release it through evaporation? _____
_____

Cool and Comfortable

Objectives   Students will determine what types of fabric absorb the most water.

Materials

4 paper cups
Marker or pen
Water
4 fabric samples
   (cotton, wool, polyester, silk)

Procedure

1. Label the paper cups as A, B, C, and D.

2. Partially fill four paper cups with exactly the same amount of water.

3. Dip a cotton fabric sample in the water in cup A. Lift the sample out of the water and allow it to drip for a few minutes over the opening of the cup (see Figure 1). When the dripping has slowed, set the cotton fabric aside. The water left in cup A will be used for comparison in step 6 of the lab.

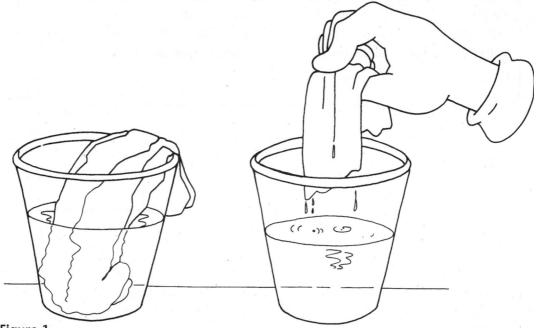

Figure 1.

4. Dip a wool fabric sample in the water in cup B. Lift the sample out of the water and allow it to drip back in the cup for a few minutes. When the dripping has slowed, set the wool fabric aside. Keep the water in cup B for analysis later in the lab.

5. Repeat step 4 for fabric samples G and D.

6. Examine the four partially filled cups of water. Determine which one contains the most water and record the letter of that cup in the Data Table under the heading "Cup with the greatest volume of water."

7. Examine the other three cups of water. Determine which one contains the second greatest volume of water and record the letter of that cup in the Data Table under the heading "Cup with the second greatest volume of water."

8. Record the letter of the cup with the third greatest volume of water in the appropriate location on the Data Table and the remaining cup beneath the heading "Cup with the least volume of water."

Data Table. Relative amounts of water in each cup.

Relative amounts of water in cups	Cup with the greatest volume of water	Cup with the second greatest volume of water	Cup with the third greatest volume of water	Cup with the least volume of water

Postlab Questions

1. Which type of fabric absorbed the most water? _____ Which type absorbed the second greatest volume of water? _____

2. If you were designing summer clothes, what fabric would you use?
_____ Why? _____
_____

3. Wool is a fabric made from the hair of sheep. It has some water repellent abilities. Why do you think that one of the natural functions of wool on sheep is to repel water? _____
_____

4. When you examine the four cups to find the type of cloth that absorbed the most water, are you looking for the cup that contains the most water, or the one that contains the least amount of water? _____

5. Why was it important that all the cloth samples be the same size?_____
_____
_____

Flipping over the Elements

Objectives

Students will familiarize themselves with the characteristics of some elements and their locations on the Periodic Table.

Time Required

60 to 90 minutes

Teaching Strategies

Before lab, make a copy of the game board for every group of three or four students. Make a copy of the Incomplete Periodic Table and Elements page for each student. Have students cut these elements into individual squares. All students in a group should stack their elements together near the game board.

To begin the game, each student places a game piece on Go! The game piece can be anything small, such as a pipe cleaner, an eraser, or a coin. Player 1 tosses four pennies on the table and moves according to the directions given on the game board. When a player lands on the square, he/she follows the directions on that square. The first player to fill in the Incomplete Periodic Table wins.

Players may want to have a periodic table similar to the one on page 13 available while they play the game.

Evaluation

Following is a suggested grading rubric:

Criteria	Points allowed	Points awarded
Prelab Questions correct	33.3	_____
Student participated in the game	33.3	_____
Postlab Questions correct	33.3	_____
Total	100	_____

Periodic Table of the Elements

Legend:
- ★ Synthetic
- ▲ Radioactive
- ( ) Indicates atomic weight of most stable isotope

Sample cell:
- 6 — Atomic Number
- Number of electrons in each shell
- C — Symbol
- Carbon — Name
- 12.01115 — Atomic Mass

| 1 / 1A | New designation / Original designation |

Group 1 / 1A
- 1 H Hydrogen 1.00797
- 3 Li Lithium 6.941
- 11 Na Sodium 22.9898
- 19 K Potassium 39.0983
- 37 Rb Rubidium 85.4678
- 55 Cs Cesium 132.905
- 87 Fr Francium (223)

Group 2 / 2A
- 4 Be Beryllium 9.0122
- 12 Mg Magnesium 24.305
- 20 Ca Calcium 40.08
- 38 Sr Strontium 87.62
- 56 Ba Barium 137.33
- 88 Ra Radium (226.0254)

Group 3 / 3B
- 21 Sc Scandium 44.956
- 39 Y Yttrium 88.905
- 57 La Lanthanum 138.91
- 89 Ac Actinium (227.0278)

Group 4 / 4B
- 22 Ti Titanium 47.88
- 40 Zr Zirconium 91.22
- 72 Hf Hafnium 178.49
- ★104 Rf Rutherfordium (261)

Group 5 / 5B
- 23 V Vanadium 50.942
- 41 Nb Niobium 92.906
- 73 Ta Tantalum 180.948
- ★105 Db Dubnium (262)

Group 6 / 6B
- 24 Cr Chromium 51.996
- 42 Mo Molybdenum 95.94
- 74 W Tungsten 183.85
- ★106 Sg Seaborgium (263)

Group 7 / 7B
- 25 Mn Manganese 54.9380
- ★43 Tc Technetium (98)
- 75 Re Rhenium 186.2
- ★107 Bh Bohrium (262)

Group 8 / 8B
- 26 Fe Iron 55.847
- 44 Ru Ruthenium 101.07
- 76 Os Osmium 190.2
- ★108 Hs Hassium (265)

Group 9 / 8B
- 27 Co Cobalt 58.9332
- 45 Rh Rhodium 102.905
- 77 Ir Iridium 192.2
- ★109 Mt Meitnerium (266)

Group 10
- 28 Ni Nickel 58.69
- 46 Pd Palladium 106.4
- 78 Pt Platinum 195.09
- ★110 Uun Ununnilium (269)

Group 11 / 1B
- 29 Cu Copper 63.54
- 47 Ag Silver 107.868
- 79 Au Gold 196.967
- ★111 Uuu Unununium (272)

Group 12 / 2B
- 30 Zn Zinc 65.37
- 48 Cd Cadmium 112.40
- 80 Hg Mercury 200.59
- ★112 Uub Ununbium (277)

Group 13 / 3A
- 5 B Boron 10.811
- 13 Al Aluminum 26.9815
- 31 Ga Gallium 69.72
- 49 In Indium 114.82
- 81 Tl Thallium 204.383
- 113 Uut

Group 14 / 4A
- 6 C Carbon 12.01115
- 14 Si Silicon 28.086
- 32 Ge Germanium 72.59
- 50 Sn Tin 118.69
- 82 Pb Lead 207.19
- 114 Uuq

Group 15 / 5A
- 7 N Nitrogen 14.0067
- 15 P Phosphorus 30.9738
- 33 As Arsenic 74.9216
- 51 Sb Antimony 121.75
- 83 Bi Bismuth 208.980
- 115 Uup

Group 16 / 6A
- 8 O Oxygen 15.9994
- 16 S Sulfur 32.064
- 34 Se Selenium 78.96
- 52 Te Tellurium 127.60
- ★84 Po Polonium (209)
- 116 Uuh

Group 17 / 7A
- 9 F Fluorine 18.9984
- 17 Cl Chlorine 35.453
- 35 Br Bromine 79.904
- 53 I Iodine 126.9044
- ★85 At Astatine (210)
- 117 Uus

Group 18 / 8A
- 2 He Helium 4.0026
- 10 Ne Neon 20.179
- 18 Ar Argon 39.948
- 36 Kr Krypton 83.80
- 54 Xe Xenon 131.29
- ★86 Rn Radon (222)
- 118 Uuo

Lanthanide series (6):
- 58 Ce Cerium 140.12
- 59 Pr Praseodymium 140.907
- 60 Nd Neodymium 144.24
- ★61 Pm Promethium (145)
- 62 Sm Samarium 150.35
- 63 Eu Europium 151.96
- 64 Gd Gadolinium 157.25
- 65 Tb Terbium 158.9254
- 66 Dy Dysprosium 162.50
- 67 Ho Holmium 164.930
- 68 Er Erbium 167.26
- 69 Tm Thulium 168.934
- 70 Yb Ytterbium 173.04
- 71 Lu Lutetium 174.97

Actinide series (7):
- 90 Th Thorium 232.038
- ★91 Pa Protactinium (231.0359)
- 92 U Uranium 238.03
- ★93 Np Neptunium (237.0482)
- ★94 Pu Plutonium (244)
- ★95 Am Americium (243)
- ★96 Cm Curium (247)
- ★97 Bk Berkelium (247)
- ★98 Cf Californium (251)
- ★99 Es Einsteinium (252)
- ★100 Fm Fermium (257)
- ★101 Md Mendelevium (258)
- ★102 No Nobelium (259)
- ★103 Lr Lawrencium (260)

Note: Elements 113-118 are not currently known. They are shown in the table at their expected positions for information only.

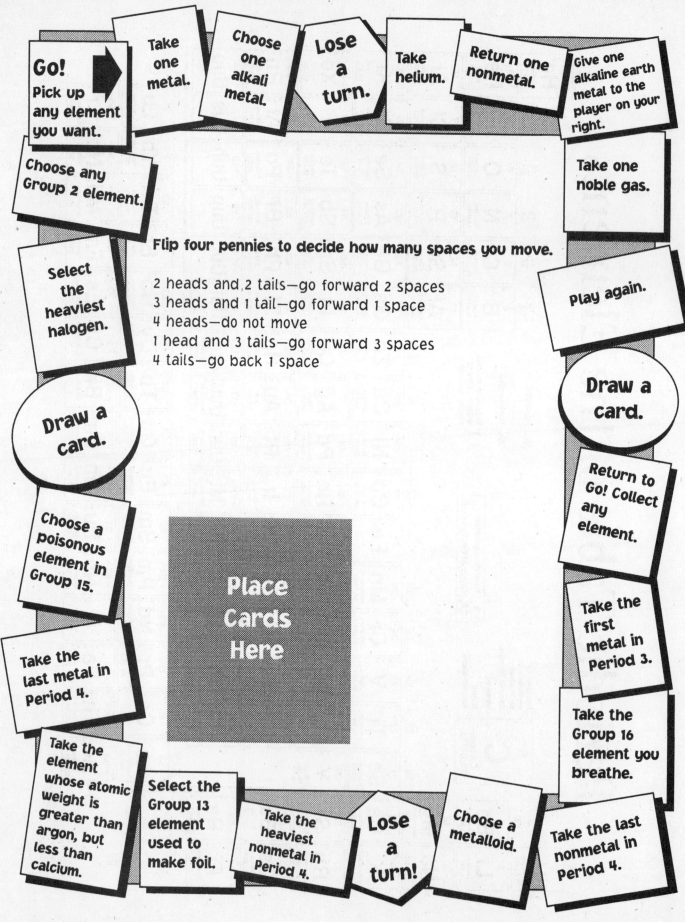

Go! Pick up any element you want.

Take one metal.

Choose one alkali metal.

Lose a turn.

Take helium.

Return one nonmetal.

Give one alkaline earth metal to the player on your right.

Take one noble gas.

Choose any Group 2 element.

Select the heaviest halogen.

Flip four pennies to decide how many spaces you move.

2 heads and 2 tails—go forward 2 spaces
3 heads and 1 tail—go forward 1 space
4 heads—do not move
1 head and 3 tails—go forward 3 spaces
4 tails—go back 1 space

Play again.

Draw a card.

Draw a card.

Choose a poisonous element in Group 15.

Place Cards Here

Return to Go! Collect any element.

Take the first metal in Period 3.

Take the last metal in Period 4.

Take the Group 16 element you breathe.

Take the element whose atomic weight is greater than argon, but less than calcium.

Select the Group 13 element used to make foil.

Take the heaviest nonmetal in Period 4.

Lose a turn!

Choose a metalloid.

Take the last nonmetal in Period 4.

......

Name_____

Incomplete Periodic Table

To win the game, collect all the missing elements and place them on the Incomplete Periodic Table. This table does not include the transition elements, found in Groups 3 through 12. Some elements are already provided for you.

1	2	13	14	15	16	17	18
				P Phosphorus			Ar Argon
					Se Selenium	Br Bromine	
Rb Rubidium		In Indium	Sn Tin	Sb Antimony	Te Tellurium		Xe Xenon
Cs Cesium	Ba Barium	Ti Thallium		Bi Bismuth	Po Polonium	As Astatine	Rn Radon
Fr Francium	Ra Radium						

© Instructional Fair • TS Denison   15   IF19310 Inexpensive Science Experiments

Elements

Cut these element cards into squares. Stack them with the other players' element cards in a convenient place near the game board.

H	Mg	Si	Cl
Hydrogen	Magnesium	Silicon	Chlorine
Li	Ca	Ge	I
Lithium	Calcium	Germanium	Iodine
Na	Sr	As	He
Sodium	Strontium	Arsenic	Helium
K	B	Pb	Ne
Potassium	Boron	Lead	Neon
Be	Al	O	N
Beryllium	Aluminum	Oxygen	Nitrogen
C	Ga	S	Kr
Carbon	Gallium	Sulfur	Krypton
		F	
		Fluorine	

Cards

Cut out the cards and stack them on the game board.

It is your lucky day— every player receives a nonmetal of his or her choice.	All living things contain this element. Take carbon.	Thank this element for making your teeth strong. Take some fluorine.
It is the most abundant element in the universe. Take hydrogen.	Salt your food and take sodium.	Kill the germs in your pool. Use some chlorine compounds.
If you cut a finger, you may need a compound made of this element. Take iodine.	If you are on a low sodium diet, you can use "lite" salt. Choose potassium.	The bad odors made by skunks contain this element. Take sulfur.
When you are at the beach, there is plenty of sand made of this element. Take silicon.	Seventy-nine percent of the atmosphere is made of this gas. Take nitrogen.	Neon signs advertise businesses. Take neon.

Flipping over the Elements

The periodic table is an impressive collection of information about the known elements. Not only does it list the elements by name and symbol, but it also gives the atomic mass and atomic number of each element. The atomic mass of an element represents the sum of protons and neutrons in its nucleus. Of the two numbers shown with each symbol, the atomic mass is always larger.

The number of protons in one atom of an element is shown in the atomic number. Logically, this is the smaller of the two numbers listed with the symbol. On the periodic table, atomic number and atomic mass increase from left to right and from top to bottom. Therefore, the lightest element, hydrogen, is located in the top left side of the table. The heaviest element, lawrencium, is in the lower right corner.

Figure 1. The atomic number of sodium is 11, and the atomic mass is rounded to 23. This means that this atom of sodium has a total of 23 protons and neutrons in its nucleus. Eleven of these are protons and 12 are neutrons.

11

Na

Sodium

22.9

All of the elements known as metals are located on the left side of the table. Nonmetals are located on the far right side of the table. Metalloids, which have characteristics of both metals and nonmetals, are found in a stair-step pattern between the metals and nonmetals.

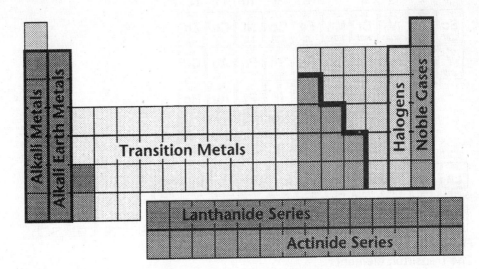

Figure 2.
Some groups of
elements are given
special names.

Each element on the periodic table is a member of a group and a period. A group is made up of all the elements in one vertical column. The numbers written at the top of a column of elements is called a *group number*. All elements in that column belong to that group. There are 18 groups in the periodic table. For example group 2 consists of beryllium, magnesium, calcium, strontium, barium, and radium. Numbers written on the left side of the periodic table before a row of elements are called the *period numbers*. Elements in that row belong to that period. There are seven periods in the periodic table. Period 2 consists of lithium, beryllium, boron, carbon, nitrogen, oxygen, fluorine, and neon.

Some groups of the elements have special names. Group 1 elements are also called the *alkali metals*. These are very reactive elements. For example, sodium and potassium may burn when they contact water. The *alkaline-earth metals*, in group 2, are very reactive, although they are not as reactive as group 1 elements.

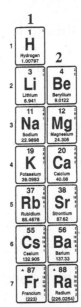

The *transition elements*, in groups 3-12, are generally very hard and dense. Iron, nickel, and copper are some common transition elements.

Group 17 elements are known as *halogens*. They are very reactive nonmetals. Group 18 elements are known as *noble* or *inert gases*. They generally do not react with other elements.

Figure 3.
The alkali and
the alkaline
earth groups

3	4	5	6	7	8	9	10	11	12
21 Sc Scandium 44.956	22 Ti Titanium 47.88	23 V Vanadium 50.942	24 Cr Chromium 51.996	25 Mn Manganese 54.9380	26 Fe Iron 55.847	27 Co Cobalt 58.9332	28 Ni Nickel 58.69	29 Cu Copper 63.54	30 Zn Zinc 65.37
39 Y Yttrium 88.905	40 Zr Zirconium 91.22	41 Nb Niobium 92.906	42 Mo Molybdenum 95.94	•43• Tc Technetium (98)	44 Ru Ruthenium 101.07	45 Rh Rhodium 102.906	46 Pd Palladium 106.4	47 Ag Silver 107.868	48 Cd Cadmium 112.40
72 Hf Hafnium 178.49	73 Ta Tantalum 180.948	74 W Tungsten 183.85	75 Re Rhenium 186.2	76 Os Osmium 190.2	77 Ir Iridium 192.2	78 Pt Platinum 195.09	79 Au Gold 196.967	80 Hg Mercury 200.59	
•104• Rf Rutherfordium (261)	•105• Db Dubnium (262)	•106• Sg Seaborgium (263)	•107• Bh Bohrium (262)	•108• Hs Hassium (265)	•109• Mt Meitnerium (266)	•110• Uun Ununnilium (269)	•111• Uuu Unununium (272)	•112• Uub Ununbium (277)	

57 La Lanthanum 138.91	58 Ce Cerium 140.12	59 Pr Praseodymium 140.907	60 Nd Neodymium 144.24	61 Pm Promethium (145)	62 Sm Samarium 150.35	63 Eu Europium 151.96	64 Gd Gadolinium 157.25	65 Tb Terbium 158.9254	66 Dy Dysprosium 162.50	67 Ho Holmium 164.930	68 Er Erbium 167.26	69 Tm Thulium 168.934	70 Yb Ytterbium 173.04	71 Lu Lutetium 174.97
89 Ac Actinium (227.0278)	90 Th Thorium 232.038	91 Pa Protactinium (231.0359)	92 U Uranium 238.03	93 Np Neptunium (237.0482)	94 Pu Plutonium (244)	95 Am Americium (243)	96 Cm Curium (247)	97 Bk Berkelium (247)	98 Cf Californium (251)	99 Es Einsteinium (252)	100 Fm Fermium (257)	101 Md Mendelevium (258)	102 No Nobelium (259)	103 Lr Lawrencium (260)

Figure 4.
The transition elements

17	18
	2 He Helium 4.0026
9 F Fluorine 18.9984	10 Ne Neon 20.179
17 Cl Chlorine 35.453	18 Ar Argon 39.948
35 Br Bromine 79.904	36 Kr Krypton 83.80
53 I Iodine 126.9044	54 Xe Xenon 131.29
•85• At Astatine (210)	•86• Rn Radon (222)

Figure 5.
The halogens and the noble gases

Prelab Questions

1. What is the *periodic table?* _____
   _____

2. In what order are the elements on the periodic table arranged? _____
   _____

3. What is the lightest element? _____

4. Elements in group 1 are also known as _____ _____.

5. Circle the correct answers. On the periodic table, metals are located on the (right, left), and the nonmetals are located on the (right, left).

6. The elements between metals and nonmetals, _____, have some characteristics of both.

7. How many groups of elements are represented on the periodic table? _____ How may periods? _____

8. What is the second element in group 1? _____ The fourth element in group 15? _____ The third element in period 3? _____

Flipping over the Elements

Objectives Students will become familiar with the characteristics of some elements and their locations on the Periodic Table.

Materials

Game board (1 per group)
Incomplete Periodic Table (1 per student)
4 pennies
Element squares
Game pieces
Game cards for the board

Procedure

1. All players place their game pieces on Go!

2. One player at a time tosses the four pennies and moves his/her playing piece according to the directions on the game board.

3. The first player to collect all of his/her elements and correctly place them on his/her Incomplete Periodic Table wins.

Postlab Questions

1. Which is heavier: lithium or sodium? _____

2. Make a statement about the atomic number of elements as you move from top to bottom of a group._____

_____

3. Which is heavier: potassium or calcium? _____

4. Make a statement about the atomic number as you move from the left to the right side of the periodic table. _____

_____

5. How many elements are in period 1? _____ period 2? _____ period 4? _____

Freeze Warning

Objectives

Students will determine how substances dissolved in water affect the freezing point of water.

Time Required

6 minutes

Teaching Strategies

Prior to the lab, have students read the Background Information and answer the Prelab Questions.

You will need access to a freezer, some dry ice, or a cooler full of ice, salt, and cold water. Lab work should be done in containers that can be set in the freezer, dry ice container, or a cooler.

Before the lab, boil water in several 500 ml containers. Place about 300 ml of water in each container (see Figure 1). Boiling is used to drive the dissolved oxygen from the water. Do not slosh or stir the boiled water. Provide each lab group with a container of boiled water at the start of the lab. The 300 ml amount will make it easy for students to divide the water into three equal amounts.

Figure 1. Boil 300 ml of water in several 500 ml containers.

Allow time for the water to cool after boiling, so students will not get burned.

Evaluation

Following is a suggested grading rubric:

Criteria	Points allowed	Points awarded
Prelab Questions correct	33.3	_____
Data Table complete	33.3	_____
Postlab Questions correct	33.3	_____
Total	100	_____

Freeze Warning

Pure water has a fixed boiling point and a fixed freezing point. It always boils at 100 degrees Celsius and freezes at 0 degrees Celsius. However, we rarely have pure water available to us because water collects minerals and pollutants as it travels over the land.

All of the substances that dissolve in water affect its freezing and boiling points. This can be very helpful to us and is one of the reasons we add certain chemicals to water.

Antifreeze is a good example of water containing another ingredient. The function of water in a car's radiator is to keep the engine cool. In the winter, this water can freeze. When water freezes, it expands and can damage its container. To keep water in a radiator from freezing and bursting it, we add "antifreeze" to the water. The antifreeze lowers water's freezing point.

There are many other substances that affect water's freezing point. Some of these substances are liquids, like antifreeze, some are solids, and others are gases.

Prelab Questions

1. What are the boiling and freezing points of pure water?_____ _____

2. How does antifreeze added to water affect its freezing point? _____

   _____

3. What would happen to a car's radiator in the winter if antifreeze were not added?

   _____

4. Why do we rarely have pure water available to us?_____

   _____

Freeze Warning

Objectives Determine how substances dissolved in water affect the freezing point of water.

Materials

Cooler or freezer
3 paper cups
Boiled water
Salt
Teaspoon
Clock
Marking pen to label the cups

Procedure

1. Label the paper cups as A, B, and C.

2. Fill cup A about one-half full of boiled water.

3. Half-fill cup B with boiled water. Now stir the water vigorously with a spoon. This stirring causes oxygen from the air to mix and dissolve in the water.

4. Half-fill cup C with boiled water. Add 1 teaspoon of salt. Stir until the salt is dissolved.

5. Place all three cups in a cooler or freezer. Note the time in the Data Table in Row 1: "Time placed in cooler."

6. Every five minutes, swirl the water in the cups to see if any has frozen to the sides. As soon as you see ice crystals, note the time in the Data Table in Row 2: "Time freezing occurred."

7. Subtract "Time placed in cooler" from "Time freezing occurred" to determine the length of time it took the water in each cup to freeze.

Data Table. Time required for water in cups A, B, and C to freeze

	Cup A Boiled water	Cup B Boiled water plus oxygen	Cup C Boiled water plus salt
1. Time placed in cooler			
2. Time freezing occurred			
3. Number of minutes required for freezing to occur			

Postlab Questions

1. In which cup did freezing occur first? _____ Last? _____

2. Which method would you recommend for lowering the freezing point of water: adding salt or adding oxygen gas? _____

_____

3. The process of boiling water drives out gases. Why did we use boiled water in this experiment? _____

_____

4. Explain how adding rock salt to ice around an ice cream churn affects the amount of time required for the ice cream to become solid.

_____

_____

Hot Wired

Objectives

Students will determine how temperature affects the length of a wire.

Time Required

50 minutes

Teaching Strategies

Prior to the lab, have students read the Background Information and answer the Prelab Questions.

Each lab group will need several inches of flexible, metal wire, a ring stand or other support to which to tie the wire, a small weight, and some ice. Hair dryers or matches are needed as heat generators. Hair dryers can be shared among groups. You may need to provide extension cords for the hair dryers if you elect to use them.

Divide the class into small groups of two or three.

Evaluation

Following is a suggested grading rubric:

Criteria	Points allowed	Points awarded
Prelab Questions correct	30	_____
Data Table complete	20	_____
Participated in lab work	20	_____
Postlab Questions correct	30	_____
Total	100	_____

Hot Wired

Everything is made of atoms, tiny particles of matter that cannot be divided. Atoms can join together to make molecules. For example, two atoms of hydrogen and one atom of oxygen combine to make a molecule of water (see Figure 1).

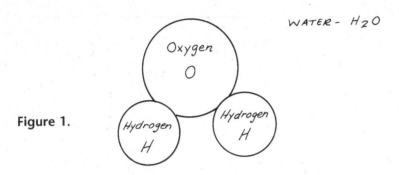

WATER - H_2O

Figure 1.

The atoms and molecules in matter are never perfectly still but are always in a state of motion. As atoms and molecules are cooled, their motion slows. Inversely, as they are warmed, they move faster.

When atoms and molecules are moving slowly, they can get very close together. That is why most materials contract as they cool. The colder they get, the more they contract. Logically, when materials are warmed, they expand. This is because molecules that are moving quickly bounce off one another with a lot of energy. This bouncing spreads the particles, and the materials expand (see Figure 2).

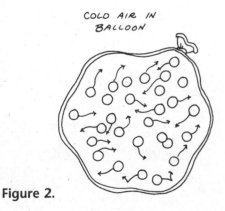

COLD AIR IN BALLOON

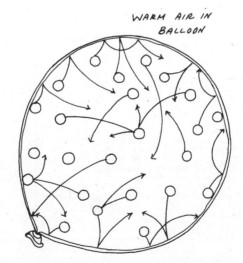

WARM AIR IN BALLOON

Figure 2.

Prelab Questions

1. What are the smallest particles of matter? _____

2. What is a water molecule? _____

3. How does cooling a material affect the motion of its atoms and molecules?

   _____

4. Warming a material causes its atoms and molecules to move faster. How does warming affect the size of a material? _____

   _____

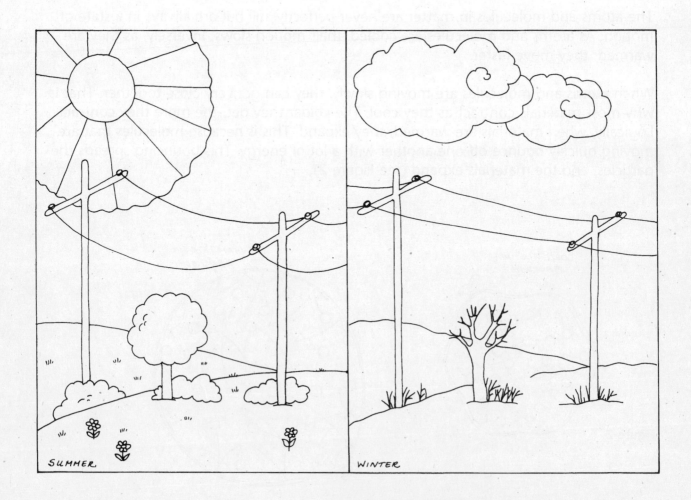

SUMMER   WINTER

Hot Wired

Objectives Students will determine how temperature affects the length of a wire.

Materials

Metal wire
Small weight
Hair dryer
Ice
Ruler
Paper towel
Ring stand

Procedure

1. Tie one end of the metal wire to a small weight.

2. Tie the other end to your desk so that the weight hangs a few centimeters above the floor (see Figure 3).

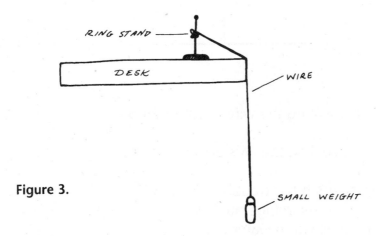

Figure 3.

3. Measure the length of the wire and record the measurement in the Data Table in column A (see Figure 4).

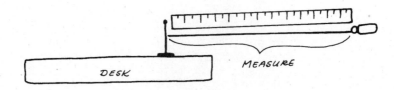

Figure 4.

4. With a hair dryer, warm the wire for five minutes.
   BE CAREFUL. A HOT WIRE CAN CAUSE A BURN.

5. Measure the length of the wire again and record your measurement in the Data Table in column B.

6. Hold an ice cube in a paper towel and rub it on the wire for five minutes.

7. Measure the length of the wire and record the measurement in the Data Table in column C.

Data Table. Length of wire

	A	B	C
Length of wire			

Postlab Questions

1. How did heating the wire affect its length?_____

2. How did cooling the wire affect its length? _____

3. Sometimes Jen has trouble removing the lid on a jar of pickles when it has been in the refrigerator. When this happens, her mom has told her to run some warm water over the lid. Why does warm water make it easier to remove the lid? _____

   _____

4. In the summer, electrical wires strung between power poles sag and hang closer to the ground. Based on what you have learned in this lab, why does this happen? _____

   _____

   _____

Just Passing Through

Objectives

Students will determine what materials will move into and out of an egg.

Time Required

25 minutes on Day 1
25 minutes on Day 2
25 minutes on Day 3

Teaching Strategies

Prior to the lab, have students read the Background Information and answer the Prelab Questions.

Each lab group will need two fresh eggs, some corn syrup, vinegar, four clear plastic cups—each large enough to hold an egg, and a triple beam balance.

Divide the class into small groups of two or three.

Evaluation

Following is a suggested grading rubric:

Criteria	Points allowed	Points awarded
Prelab Questions correct	20	_____
Data Table complete	30	_____
Participated in lab work	20	_____
Postlab Questions correct	30	_____
Total	100	_____

Just Passing Through

Many cells are covered by a membrane. This membrane allows substances to enter and exit the cell. Some chemicals pass through the cell membrane easier than others. When a cell is placed in a liquid environment, certain materials in the liquid environment may enter the cell. Certain materials from inside the cell may leave the cell and pass into the liquid environment. This passage of material is determined by the cell membrane.

The liquid environment outside of a cell is composed of liquid and the solid materials dissolved in the liquid. The liquid holding the dissolved solid materials is called the *solvent,* and the dissolved particles in the liquid are known as the *solute.* The cell is also composed of liquid material with certain solids dissolved in it.

When the concentration of solute in a cell is lower than the concentration of solute in the environment outside the cell, water will leave the cell. If the concentration of solute in the cell is greater than the concentration of solute outside of the cell, water will move into the cell.

The process whereby materials pass into and out of a cell is called *diffusion.* Diffusion is the passage of materials from a place of greater concentration to a place of lesser concentration (see Figure 1).

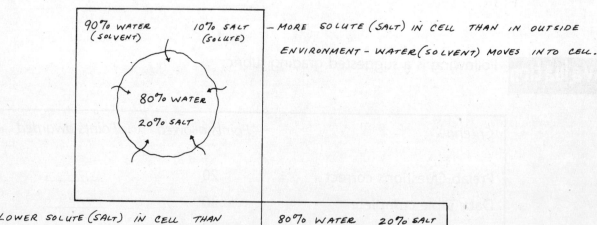

Figure 1.

Prelab Questions

1. What is *diffusion*? _____
_____

2. What causes materials to enter and exit a cell? _____
_____

3. What is the difference in a solute and a solvent? _____
_____
_____

4. Is water a solute or a solvent? _____

5. What composes the environment outside the cell? _____
_____
_____

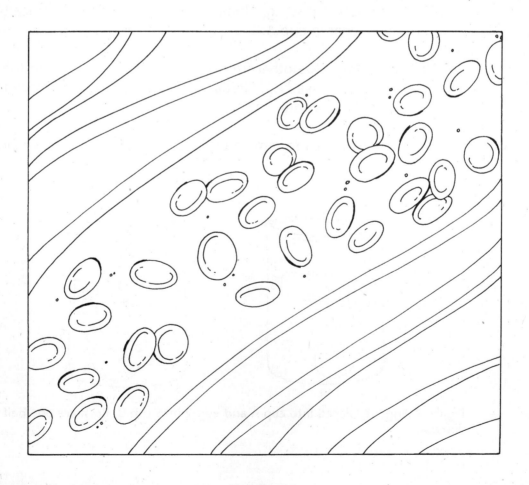

Just Passing Through

Objectives Students will determine what materials will move into and out of an egg.

Materials

Two fresh eggs
Vinegar
Corn syrup
Triple beam balance
Four clear cups (large enough for the egg)
Black marking pen
Paper towels

Procedure Day 1

1. Use a marking pen and label one plastic cup as "A" and the other cup as "B."

2. Fill both cups about one-half full of vinegar.

3. Find the mass of one of the fresh eggs and record its mass in the Data Table beside the heading, "Initial mass" under "Egg 1." Place this egg into the vinegar in cup A.

4. Find the mass of the other fresh egg and record its mass in the Data Table beside the heading, "Initial mass" under "Egg 2." Place this egg in the vinegar in cup B.

5. Allow the two cups to remain undisturbed for 24 hours (see Figure 2).

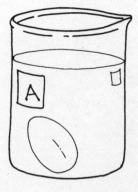 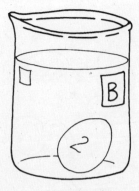

Figure 2. Egg 1 is placed into cup A and egg 2 into cup B. Both are one-half full of vinegar.

Day 2
1. Remove the egg from cup A and rinse it with water. Very gently dry the egg with a paper towel.

2. Find the mass of egg 1 and record its mass beside the heading, "Mass after vinegar" under "Egg 1." Place this egg in front of cup A so you will not get it confused with egg 2.

3. Repeat step 2 for the egg in cup B. Record its mass beside the heading, "Mass after vinegar" under "Egg 2." Place this egg in front of cup B.

4. Label two paper cups as C and D.

5. Fill one half of cup C with distilled water and one half of cup D with syrup.

6. Place egg 1 into cup C containing water and place egg 2 into cup D containing syrup.

7. Leave the two cups undisturbed for 24 hours (see Figure 3).

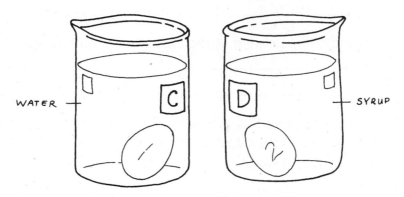

Figure 3. After the eggs are rinsed, dried, and weighed, egg 1 is placed into cup C and egg 2 into cup D. Cup C is one-half full of distilled water and cup D is one-half full of syrup.

Day 3
1. Remove the egg from cup C and towel dry gently. Observe the appearance of the egg. Find the mass of the egg and record this beside the heading, "Mass after last 24 hours (in water)."

2. Remove the egg from cup D, rinse with water, and towel dry gently. Observe the appearance of the egg. Find the mass of the egg and record this beside the heading, "Mass after last 24 hours (in syrup)."

3. Answer the Postlab Questions.

Data Table. Mass of the two eggs.

	Egg 1	Egg 2
Initial mass		
Mass after vinegar		
Mass after last 24 hours	(in water)	(in syrup)

1. What effect did vinegar have on both of the eggs? _____

   _____

2. Describe the appearance of the egg after it soaks in water for 24 hours. _____

   _____

3. Describe the appearance of the egg after it soaks in syrup for 24 hours. _____

   _____

4. An egg is surrounded by a membrane. Inside the egg is the white that consists of water and dissolved protein. The yolk, inside the egg, is filled with fat and water. Syrup is sugar dissolved in water.

   a. Use the information above to describe whether water diffused out of or into the egg placed in syrup. Explain your answer. _____

      _____

   b. Use the information above to describe whether water diffused out of or into the egg that soaked overnight in distilled water. Explain your answer. _____

      _____

5. What was the importance of finding the mass of the egg each time?

   _____

   What do changes in mass indicate? _____

I Sense Some Friction Here

Objectives

Students will analyze the effect of friction on the forces required to slide a block of wood.

Time Required

50 minutes

Teaching Strategies

Prior to the lab, have students read the Background Information and answer the Prelab Questions.

Collect blocks of wood, so each group of two or three students has one. The size of the wood does not matter, except it should be small enough to move around. It should have a rough surface if possible. You can rough up the surface prior to the lab using a hammer or saw.

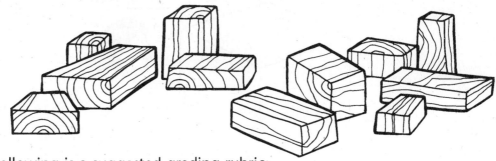

Evaluation

Following is a suggested grading rubric:

Criteria	Points allowed	Points awarded
Prelab Questions correct	33.3	_____
Data Table complete	33.3	_____
Postlab Questions correct	33.3	_____
Total	100	_____

I Sense Some Friction Here

Throughout the day you experience various pushes and pulls. You push a pencil when you complete your homework. You pull a book out of your book bag when you start class. A push and a pull is called a *force*.

Objects are affected by forces. Forces change the motion of an object. One force can cancel the effects of another force. Think about a football player running the ball up the field. He continues forward until a player from the other team tackles him and stops his motion. The force of the defensive player's tackle stops the motion of the running back. Only when forces are unbalanced will motion continue.

When two surfaces are in contact with each other, a special force must be considered. This force is called *friction*. Friction opposes motion. When you push a heavy box across a rough floor, the floor seems to grab onto and prevent the box from being moved. In order for you to slide the box forward, you must find a way to overcome friction (see Figure 1).

Figure 1.

Friction is not always the same. The amount of friction between two surfaces depends on the materials that make up the surfaces, the texture of the surfaces, and how tightly the surfaces are pushed together. Pushing a heavy box across carpet is harder than pushing it across a polished wooden floor. Friction is greater with the carpet than the wooden floor.

Friction can be reduced by changing the texture of a surface. You can reduce friction by smoothing the texture. This can be done by sanding, oiling, or greasing a surface. Oiling the gears of a bicycle helps to reduce friction and to make the ride easier.

Prelab Questions

1. Define *force*. _____
   _____

2. Explain how friction and motion are related. _____
   _____

3. Explain why you are more likely to slide down when standing on an icy surface than when standing on a dry surface._____
   _____
   _____

4. Describe some ways you can reduce friction. _____
   _____
   _____

5. List three factors that determine the amount of friction between two surfaces.
   _____
   _____
   _____

I Sense Some Friction Here

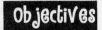 **Objectives** Analyze the effect of friction on the forces required to slide a block of wood.

Materials

Block of wood
Large rubber band
Large staple or small nail
Hammer
Ruler
Tape
Sand paper
Oil

Procedure 1. Attach a rubber band to a block of wood with a nail or a large staple (see Figure 2).

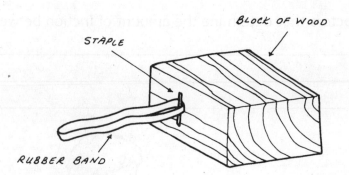

Figure 2.

2. Select a surface over which you can pull the block of wood by the rubber band.

3. Without stretching the rubber band, measure the length of the rubber band. Record the length of the rubber band in cm in the Data Table beside "Initial measurement of rubber band."

4. Place the block on the surface you selected and gently pull on the rubber band until the block begins to move. Measure the length of the rubber band when it gently moves the block. Record that measurement beside "Gentle pull on regular surface" in the Data Table (see Figure 3).

5. Pick up the block of wood and sand the bottom of the block.

Place the sanded surface of the block on the surface you will pull the block over. Gently pull on the rubber band until the block begins to move. Measure the length of the rubber band when it is able to gently move the block. Record that measurement beside "Gentle pull on sanded surface" in the Data Table.

6. Pick up the block of wood and generously rub oil along the underside of the block. Place the oiled side of the block on the surface over which the block will move and gently pull on the rubber band until the block moves. Measure the length of the rubber band at the point at which the block begins to move. Record that measurement beside "Gentle pull on oiled surface" in the Data Table.

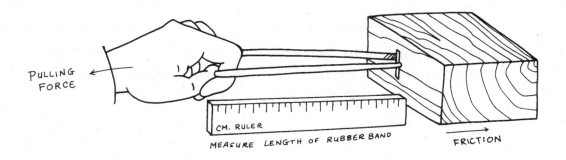

PULLING FORCE

CM. RULER

MEASURE LENGTH OF RUBBER BAND

FRICTION

Figure 3. Measure the length of the rubber band at the point where the block begins to slide on the surface.

Data Table. Length of rubber band at various forms of friction

	Length of rubber band (cm)
Initial measurement of rubber band	
Gentle pull on regular surface	
Gentle pull on sanded surface	
Gentle pull on oiled surface	

1. When was there the greatest stretch in the rubber band? _____

2. As friction increases, does length of the rubber band increase or decrease? _____ Explain your answer.

   _____

   _____

3. What would be the purpose of oil on parts of machines? _____

   _____

4. What causes a bobsled to go faster on a snowy hill than on a hill made of dirt? _____

   _____

5. At what point in the experiment would you say friction was the greatest between the block and surface over which it moved? _____ At what point was friction the least? _____

It's a Stick Up!

Objectives Students will compare the flexibility of different types of polymers.

Time Required

60 minutes

Teaching Strategies

Prior to the lab, have students read the Background Information and answer the Prelab Questions.

Collect several different kinds of plastic sacks—grocery sacks, dry-cleaning sacks, garbage sacks, food sacks, etc.

Buy some wooden skewers from the outdoor cooking section of the grocery store. Long dissecting needles can be substituted.

Divide the class into small groups of two or three.

Evaluation Following is a suggested grading rubric:

Criteria	Points allowed	Points awarded
Prelab Questions correct	20	_____
Participated in lab work	20	_____
Data Table complete	30	_____
Postlab Questions correct	30	_____
Total	100	_____

It's a Stick Up!

Plastic is a man-made substance created from raw materials such as crude oil and coal. Chemically, plastic is described as a *polymer*. A polymer is a long chain of repeating units. One way to visualize the structure of a polymer is to look at a string of pop beads. In this analogy, the string of beads is the polymer, and the individual beads are repeating units.

In plastic polymers, the repeating units are *carbon atoms*. Therefore, you can accurately say that a plastic polymer is a long chain of carbon atoms. The unique properties of different plastics are due to the atoms that are connected to these carbon atoms.

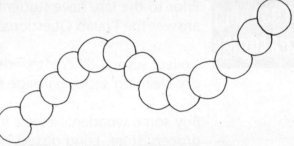

Figure 1. A polymer can be compared to a string of beads. Each repeating unit is represented by one bead.

Depending on the intended use of the plastic, the polymers in the plastic might be free to move around, or they might be rigidly fixed in place. If they are free to move, the plastic is flexible. The individual polymers in flexible plastics can move aside when under stress. However, in rigid plastics, polymers cannot move. Under stress they break and create a hole.

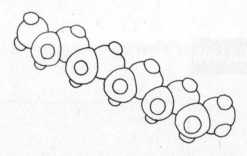

Figure 2. Plastics are made of polymers of carbon atoms.

To test the flexibility of a polymer, hold a portion of a plastic sack in your hands and gently pull it in opposite directions. Most likely, you will cause the plastic to stretch.

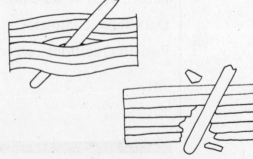

Figure 3. In flexible plastic, polymers move aside when a pin is inserted. However, a pin causes a break to occur in inflexible polymers.

The ability to stretch indicates that the polymers are flexible.

Figure 4. Hold a piece of plastic sack in both hands, and pull in opposite directions.

When plastic stretches, some of the polymer chains move from one area of the plastic to another. In other words, you pull polymer chains out of their normal position into a "lip" formed by the stretching process. This would be impossible to do if the polymers were held rigidly in place.

There are many kinds and qualities of plastic on the market. Some are more flexible than others. The flexibility of a plastic helps determine its use: some plastic sacks are designed to hold trash, while others are used to store food. Plastic sacks have also been created to hold laundry, groceries, fast food, and beverages.

Figure 5. Some uses of plastic sacks

Prelab Questions

1. What is *plastic?* _____

2. What is a *polymer?* _____

   Of what atoms are plastic polymers made? _____

   _____

3. In the analogy of a string of pop beads as a polymer, what represents the individual repeating units? _____

4. What can you say about the polymers in a stretchable plastic sack? _____

   _____

It's a Stick Up!

Objectives Compare the flexibility of different types of polymers.

Materials

Plastic sacks (6 different types)
Labels
Wooden skewer
Vegetable oil
Beaker
Clear tape

Procedure

1. Label six types of plastic sacks as A, B, C, D, E, and F.

2. Fill one of the plastic sacks with water. If it has a leak, place tape over the leak to seal it.

3. Dip the pointed end of the skewer into vegetable oil.

4. Hold the sack of water over a large beaker. Very slowly, insert the skewer into the sack, using a twisting motion (see Figure 6). If water escapes, collect it in the beaker.

Figure 6. Slowly insert a skewer into the plastic sack of water.

5. In the Data Table, record the amount of water that escaped when you skewered the bag.

6. Based on your experimental results, complete the second and third columns of the Data Table.

7. Repeat steps 2-5 with the other plastic sacks. Record your results in the Data Table.

Data Table. Volume of water lost during the skewer process

	Amount of water lost during skewering process	Is the polymer flexible and stretchable? (yes or no)	Types of items this type of plastic could be used to hold:
Plastic Sack A			
Plastic Sack B			
Plastic Sack C			
Plastic Sack D			
Plastic Sack E			
Plastic Sack F			

Postlab Questions

1. Which type of plastic sack contains the most flexible polymers? _____ How do you know? _____
_____

2. You are a plastic designer for a milk company. You have been assigned the job of selecting a type of plastic sack that can hold a pint of milk in a lunch box. Based on your results today, which type of plastic would be best for this job: A, B, C, D, E, or F? _____ Why?
_____
_____

3. If no water escaped from a plastic sack when it was skewered, what does that tell you about the polymers in that sack? _____
_____

Metric Matters

Objectives
Students will measure microscopic lengths on a penny using the stereo microscope.

Time Required

60 minutes

Teaching Strategies

Prior to the lab, have students read the Background Information and answer the Prelab Questions.

Make rulers for this lab by photocopying a ruler onto paper or transparency film. The transparent rulers work best.

Divide the class into small groups of two or three.

As an introductory activity, have students examine meter sticks and locate the centimeter markings and millimeter markings. Students should measure a few classroom items with the meter stick, such as the height of a student, the width of the room, the length of a dollar bill, or the width of their finger.

Explain how to use the stereo microscope. Point out the low and high focus, as well as the lighting.

Evaluation
Following is a suggested grading rubric:

Criteria	Points allowed	Points awarded
Prelab Questions correct	20	_____
Data Table complete	30	_____
Drawing of "tail" side of penny	20	_____
Postlab Questions correct	30	_____
Total	100	_____

Metric Matters

How tall are you? When you think of your height, do you think in feet and inches, or meters and centimeters? Chances are, you are more familiar with the measurement system that uses feet and inches. This is called the English system, and is the one most commonly used in the United States.

In many countries, the metric system is used every day. In the metric system, the basic unit of length is the meter. A meter is a little longer than a yard. Units for measuring long distances are 10, 100, or 1,000 times as long as a meter. For example, many road signs in Europe and Canada post the distance to the next town in kilometers. One kilometer is 1,000 meters.

In the metric system, small distances or lengths are measured in tenths, hundredths, or thousandths of meters. For example, one hundredth of a meter is a centimeter. In other words, there are 100 centimeters in a meter. A smaller measure of length, a millimeter, is one thousandth of a meter. There are 1,000 millimeters in a meter. This means that there are 10 millimeters in 1 centimeter.

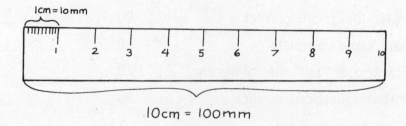

Figure 1. There are 10 millimeters in one centimeter. Millimeters and centimeters are used to measure small lengths.

Sometimes scientists measure distances that are so small they must be measured under the microscope. Using a small paper or transparent ruler, you can accurately determine microscopic lengths.

Prelab Questions

1. What system of measurement do we use in the United States? _____

2. What system of measurement do people in Canada and Europe use? _____

3. Which is longer, a meter or a yard? _____

4. What do we call the length of measurement that is one hundredth of a meter? _____ Name something that is a centimeter long. _____

5. What do we call the length of measurement that is one thousandth of a meter? _____ Name something that is a millimeter long. _____

6. How long is the ruler in the drawing below in centimeters? _____ In millimeters? _____

7. In the metric system, what unit of length is used to measure distances between cities? _____ How many meters does this unit equal? _____

Metric Matters

Objectives Measure microscopic lengths on a penny using the stereo microscope.

Materials
Stereo microscope
Penny
Transparent or paper metric ruler
Forceps

Procedure

1. Without the aid of the microscope, measure the width of the penny as accurately as possible. Record that measurement in the Data Table.

2. Measure the thickness of the penny as accurately as possible. Record the measurement in the Data Table.

3. Place the penny head's side up under the stereo microscope and turn on the microscope light.

4. With the microscope on low power, look in the eyepiece. Move the penny into the center of your field of view.

5. Focus on the penny and ruler. As accurately as possible, measure the width of the penny, the width of the date, and the height of Abraham Lincoln's ear. Enter those measurements in the Data Table.

6. Change the microscope focus to high power, and repeat step 5.

7. Hold the penny on its side with forceps. With the microscope on high power, use the transparent ruler to measure the thickness of the penny. Record the measurement in the Data Table.

8. Repeat step 7 with the microscope focused on low power.

9. Turn the penny over so that the tail's side is up and view on low power. Draw this side of the penny in the box, showing as much detail as possible.

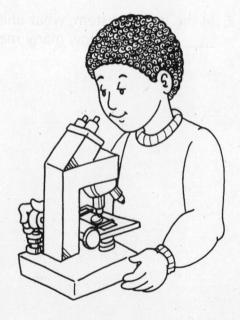

Data Table. Metric measurements of the penny

	Width of penny	Thickness of penny	Width of date	Height of Abraham Lincoln's ear
Penny not under microscope				
Penny under low power				
Penny under high power				

Drawing of tail's side of penny on low power

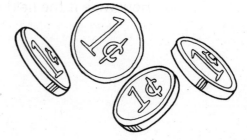

1. Which way were you able to measure the penny most accurately: without the microscope, with the microscope on low power, or with the microscope on high power? _____

2. When you look through the microscope, the area that you see is called the *field of view*. Does the field of view cover more area on low power or on high power? _____

3. The very short distance between two millimeter marks can be divided into ten spaces. Could you measure such short distances using the microscope? _____ Explain how. _____

   _____

   _____

4. Name five other objects whose details you might measure under the stereo microscope. _____

   _____

5. Examine the following drawing that shows a microscope's field of view. Answer the following questions about this drawing.

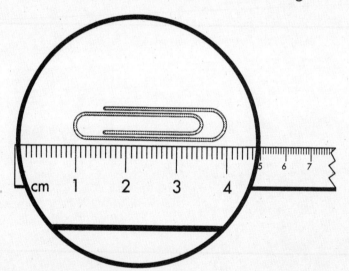

   a. How long is the paper clip? _____

   b. How wide is the field of view? _____

Out in Space

Objectives
Students will demonstrate that space exists between particles of a solid and a liquid.

Time Required
30 minutes

Teaching Strategies
Prior to the lab, have students read the Background Information and answer the Prelab Questions.

Divide the class into groups of two or three.

Evaluation
Following is a suggested grading rubric:

Criteria	Points allowed	Points awarded
Prelab Questions correct	25	_____
Groups on task during the lab	20	_____
Activity sheet completed correctly	25	_____
Postlab Questions correct	30	_____
Total	100	_____

Out in Space

Matter is anything that has mass and takes up space. The three most familiar states of matter are solids, liquids, and gases. These states are called *phases*. The particles of matter in each phase are arranged differently. These different arrangements affect the range of motion of each state (see Figure 1).

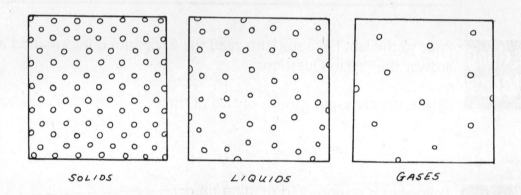

SOLIDS   LIQUIDS   GASES

Figure 1.

Solids have a definite shape and volume. This is because the particles that make up a solid are packed tightly. These particles can move slightly, but they cannot really change their position. You and your desk are examples of solids, due to your orderly arrangement of particles.

Liquids have a definite volume, but no definite shape. Liquid particles slide over one another and will take the shape of the container in which they are placed. Water assumes the shape of the glass in which it is poured. The particles of a liquid are close together, but move enough so they do not stay in a fixed position.

Gases have no definite shape and no definite volume. They will take the shape of any container in which they are placed. But unlike a liquid, gases expand to fill available space. If you open a bottle of perfume in the front of the room, it will not be long until people in the back of the room can smell the perfume. This is because gases expand and fill the volume of the room. Particles in a gas can move far from one another.

When the concentration of solute in a cell is lower than the concentration of solute in the environment outside the cell, water will leave the cell. If the concentration of solute in the cell is greater than the concentration of solute outside of the cell, water will move into the cell.

Prelab Questions

1. What are the three phases of matter? _____

2. In a phase, what determines the movement of particles? _____
   _____

3. Explain the difference between a liquid and a gas. _____
   _____
   _____

4. Of the three phases, which one moves slightly but does not change position?
   _____

5. Is there any space between the particles that make up a solid? _____
   Explain your answer. _____
   _____

Out in Space

Objectives Students will determine whether space exists between the particles of a solid and particles of a liquid.

Materials

Sand
Marbles
Rubbing alcohol
Spoon
5 beakers (250 ml)

Procedure

1. Fill one beaker to the 250-ml mark with marbles.

2. Fill a second beaker to the 250-ml mark with sand.

3. Record the volume of sand in Data Table 1 as 250 ml under the heading "Starting volume."

4. Observe the space between the marbles in beaker 1 and the space between the sand particles in beaker 2.

5. Pour sand from beaker 2 into beaker 1 until you can add no more without going over the 250-ml mark. Stir periodically with a spoon as you add the sand.

6. Look at beaker 2 and record in Data Table 1 the volume of sand that remains in it after pouring part of it into beaker 1. This number should be placed under the heading "Remaining volume."

7. Fill a third beaker to the 250-ml mark with water. Record the starting volume of beaker 3 as 250 ml under the heading "Starting volume."

8. Slowly pour water from beaker 3 into beaker 1 (the one with the marbles and sand) until no more water can be placed in the beaker without exceeding the 250-ml mark.

9. Look at beaker 3 and record in Data Table 1 the volume of water that remains in beaker 3 after pouring part of it into beaker 1. This number should be placed under the heading "Remaining volume."

10. Place 125 ml of water into beaker 4 and 125 ml of rubbing alcohol into beaker 5.

11. Record the starting volumes of beaker 4 and 5 as 125 ml in Data Table 2.

12. Slowly pour all the water from beaker 4 into beaker 5, and stir.

13. Record the combined volume of beaker 4 and 5 in Data Table 2 under "Combined volume."

14. Dispose of the materials in your beakers as indicated by the teacher and answer the Postlab Questions.

Data Table 1. Beakers 2 and 3 results

Beaker	Starting volume	Remaining volume
2 (sand)		
3 (water)		

Data Table 2. Beakers 4 and 5 results

Beaker	Starting volume	Combined volume
4 (water)		
5 (alcohol)		

1. Was there more empty space visible around the marbles or the sand before combining them?_____

_____

2. Was there more empty space visible around the sand or water before combining them? _____

_____

3. Subtract the remaining volume of sand in beaker 2 from the starting volume of sand to determine the volume (mL) that exists between the marbles in beaker 1. Show your work below.

4. Subtract the remaining volume of water in beaker 3 from the starting volume of water to determine the volume (mL) that exists between the sand particles in beaker 2. Show your work below.

5. To find the volume of space between the particles of alcohol in beaker 5, subtract the combined volume from 250 ml. Show your work below.

6. Based on your results, is there space between particles in a solid? _____ Is there space between particles in a liquid? _____ Support your answer. _____

_____

_____

Penny Pushers

Objectives

Students will demonstrate how energy is transferred from one object to another.

Time Required

50 minutes

Teaching Strategies

Prior to the lab, have students read the Background Information and answer the Prelab Questions.

Divide the class into small groups of three or four.

Prior to the lab, collect enough pennies so that each group has ten pennies.

Evaluation

Following is a suggested grading rubric:

Criteria	Points allowed	Points awarded
Prelab Questions correct	30	_____
Groups on task during the lab	20	_____
Activity sheet completed correctly	20	_____
Postlab Questions correct	30	_____
Total	100	_____

Penny Pushers

When you play miniature golf, how does the golf ball get energy? Of course, it comes from your swinging the golf club. You move your arms and strike the ball with the club. The ball receives the amount of energy equal to the force with which you moved your arms. Energy is transferred from your arms to the golf club and then to the golf ball.

Have you ever witnessed a car accident where a parked car was struck from behind by a moving car? If you have, you probably remember how the parked car lunged forward once it was hit. The distance the parked car moved was equal to the force the moving car exerted on it. During the collision, energy was transferred from the moving to the parked car.

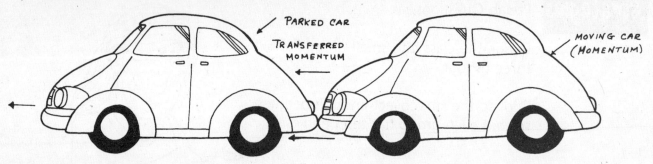

Figure 1. As a moving car collides with a parked car, the parked car moves forward. The distance of movement is equal to the intensity of the collision.

A moving car has *momentum*. Momentum is the product of a body's mass and velocity. A bowling ball rolling down a hill would have more momentum than a basketball rolling down a hill. A moving object will have a large momentum if it has a large mass, a large velocity, or both. The momentum of an object will not change unless the velocity or the mass changes. As mentioned in the examples above, momentum can be transferred from one object to another. The momentum of the moving car was transferred to the parked car. The momentum of your arms swinging the golf club was transferred to the golf ball by the way of the golf club. When an object keeps or transfers momentum, that object follows the law of conservation of momentum. Momentum is never destroyed; it is only transferred from one object to another.

Prelab Questions

1. Describe *the law of conservation of momentum*. _____

   _____

2. What two factors influence the momentum transferred from one object to another?

   _____

3 a. Imagine that a small car was stopped at a red light waiting for the light to change colors. Explain how momentum will influence the parked car if it is hit from behind by a large truck. _____

_____

  b. Explain how momentum will influence the parked car if it is hit from behind by another small car. _____

_____

4. Explain how striking a billiard ball with the cue ball in pool is an example of conservation of momentum. _____

_____

5. Give an example of conservation of momentum.

_____

_____

Penny Pushers

Objectives   Students will demonstrate how
energy is transferred from one object
to another.

Materials

10 pennies
Meter stick

Procedure

1. Select a level place on the floor or on a long table.

2. Place the meter stick on the table or floor so that the cm side is facing upward. Place one penny flat on the table so that it is barely touching the meter stick at the 1-cm mark. This penny will represent a small car that will be set into motion.

3. Place another penny flat on the table next to the 15-cm mark on the meter stick so that it barely touches the meter stick (see Figure 2). This penny will represent a small, parked car.

4. With your finger, gently push the penny at the 1-cm mark so that it moves forward and strikes the penny at the 15-cm mark. You may need to do this several times until you get a collision. This will represent a small car that is traveling slowly striking a parked car. In Data Table 1 beside "1 penny striking 1 penny softly," record the distance the penny at the 15-cm mark traveled from its starting point.

5. Repeat step 3, but this time, push the penny at the 1-cm mark with a strong force so that it moves quickly toward the second penny. This will represent a small car that is traveling at a high rate of speed striking a small parked car. In Data Table 1, record the distance the second penny traveled from the 15-cm mark. Mark your distance beside "1 penny striking 1 penny strongly."

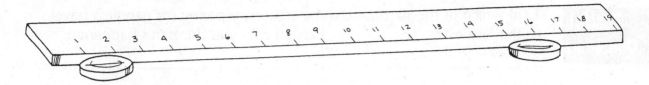

Figure 2. The position of the two pennies next to the meter stick.

6. Place one penny at the 1-cm mark and two pennies starting at the 15-cm mark. The two pennies at the 15-cm mark should be touching each other (see Figure 3).

7. Lightly push the 1-cm penny toward the two pennies so that a collision occurs. Record the distances the pennies from the 15-cm mark moved from their starting point in the Data Table next to "'1 penny striking 2 pennies softly." Repeat this step again, but this time, push the one penny with a strong force. Record your measurements in Data Table 1 next to "1 penny striking 2 pennies strongly."

Figure 3.

8. For the last two trials, place two pennies that touch each other at the 1-cm mark and six pennies that touch at the 15-cm mark. Lightly push the two pennies so they strike the six pennies. In "2 pennies striking 6 pennies softly," record the distance the pennies traveled from the 15-cm point. Repeat this once again, but this time, push the two pennies with a greater force. Record your measurements beside "2 pennies striking 6 pennies strongly" in Data Table 1.

Data Table 1. Results of penny collisions

	Distance pennies traveled from 15-cm mark
1 penny striking 1 penny softly	
1 penny striking 1 penny strongly	
1 penny striking 2 pennies softly	
1 penny striking 2 pennies strongly	
2 pennies striking 6 pennies softly	
2 pennies striking 6 pennies strongly	

1. In which of the six trials did the stationary penny (or pennies) travel the farthest? _____ Explain why you think this happened.

   _____

2. Did the speed of the penny or pennies at the 1-cm mark influence the distance that the stationary pennies traveled? _____ Explain. _____

   _____

3. Which of the six trials would be representative of a small car striking a car twice its size at a high rate of speed?_____

4. Which of the six trials would be representative of a small car striking a car three times its size at a low rate of speed? _____

5. What two things in this lab influenced the distance the stationary penny or pennies moved? _____

   _____

6. Explain why some people are hesitant to drive small cars on the open road. _____

   _____

   _____

Ticked Off

Objectives

Students will demonstrate how sound travels differently through solids and gases.

Time Required

50 minutes

Teaching Strategies

Prior to the lab, have students read the Background Information and answer the Prelab Questions.

Divide the class into small groups of three or four.

This activity is best done outside so that students do not get confused by sounds made by different lab groups.

Evaluation

Following is a suggested grading rubric:

Criteria	Points allowed	Points awarded
Prelab Questions correct	33.3	_____
Groups on task during the lab	33.3	_____
Postlab Questions correct	33.3	_____
Total	100	_____

Ticked Off

Indians used to put an ear on the ground to listen for the sound of approaching horse hooves. They could hear the horse hooves through the ground, but not through the air. Sound is caused by vibration of molecules. Vibrations travel at different speeds through different media.

Most solids transmit sound or vibrations better than gases. This is because of the action of the molecules in the solid. When a sound is made, molecules vibrate. The molecules of a solid are packed tightly together. When a molecule vibrates, it bumps into other molecules in the solid. The vibrations then pass from one molecule to another. This happens quickly. Vibrations are passed more quickly through a solid than a liquid. In a liquid the molecules are not packed together as tightly as the molecules are in a solid (see Figure 1).

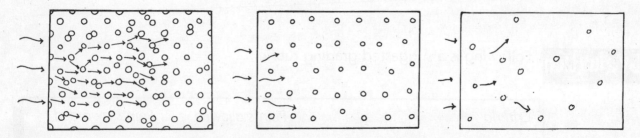

Figure 1. The molecules of a solid transmit vibrations better than the molecules of a liquid because of how closely the solid's molecules are packed to one another. Vibrations are carried more slowly through a gas than through a liquid.

Gas molecules are farther apart than the molecules of a liquid. The vibrating molecules have farther to travel before they bump into other molecules of the gas. Vibrations are carried more slowly through a gas than through a liquid (see Figure 1).

Other things can also affect the speed at which a sound wave travels. Molecules move more quickly in warm temperatures than in cold temperatures. This causes the sound waves to travel quickly.

Prelab Questions

1. Why does sound travel more quickly in solids than in liquids? _____
   _____

2. Why does sound travel more quickly in liquids than in gases? _____
   _____

3. Besides the media through which the sound travels, what else can affect the speed at which sound travels? _____

4. Explain why sound might be louder on a foggy day than on a clear day. _____
   _____
   _____

Ticked Off

Objectives Students will demonstrate how sound travels differently through solids and gases.

Materials

Meter stick
Ticking watch or clock

Procedure

1. When you begin this activity, make certain you are not positioned very close to other lab groups. This will prevent noises from their groups from influencing your results. One person in the lab group should sit down and close his or her eyes. Hold the ticking watch to the person's ear and allow him or her to hear what the watch sounds like. Walk one meter from the seated person. Ask if the person hears the ticking of the watch. If "no," slowly walk toward him or her until the person indicates the ticking watch can be heard. As soon as the watch can be heard, measure the distance you are from the person's head. Record your measurement in cm in Data Table 1 under "Distance sound is heard through a gas." Record this information in the row beside the name of the seated person.

2. Repeat step 1 with all members of the lab group. Record the results beside each name in Data Table 1.

3. One person in the lab group should sit down and close his/her eyes. Place a meter stick against the back of the seated person's ear. Place the ticking watch on the opposite end of the meter stick from the person's ear (see Figure 3). Ask if the person hears the ticking watch at the end of the meter stick. If so, record the distance of the watch from the ear as one meter in the Data Table. If he/she cannot hear the ticking sound, slowly push the watch up the meter stick toward his/her ear until he/she hears the ticking. Record the number of "cm" at which this occurs in Data Table 1 under "Distance sound is heard through a solid."

Figure 3.

4. Repeat step 3 with all group members and record their distances in Data Table 1.

Data Table 1. Distance sound travels

Group members	Distance sound is heard through a gas	Distance sound is heard through a solid
1.		
2.		
3.		

Postlab Questions

1. Find the average distance sound is heard through a gas for your group by adding results in the second column and dividing by the number of people in your group. Show your work below.

2. Find the average distance sound is heard through a solid for your group by adding results in the third column and dividing by the number of people in your group. Show your work below.

3. Does sound travel more quickly through a solid or a gas? _____

4. If we had performed this activity under water, predict how the results would have compared with the results you obtained in the lab today.

_____

_____

Would You Prefer Paper or Plastic?

Objectives

Students will compare the mass of paper and plastic sacks and the amount of space they occupy.

Time Required

60 minutes

Teaching Strategies

Prior to the lab, have students read the Background Information and answer the Prelab Questions.

Collect a variety of sacks used in grocery stores. Point out that landfill space is at a premium, and disposable materials that use up little of that space are preferable to those that occupy a lot of space. However, landfill space is not the only consideration in choosing a disposable product.

Divide the class into small groups of twos or threes.

As an introductory activity, have students count the number of paper sacks they can stuff into a shoe box and close the lid. Then have them do the same thing with plastic sacks. This will give them some idea of the concept they are exploring in the lab.

Evaluation

Following is a suggested grading rubric:

Criteria	Points allowed	Points awarded
Prelab Questions correct	33.3	_____
Data Table complete	33.3	_____
Postlab Questions correct	33.3	_____
Total	100	_____

Would You Prefer Paper or Plastic?

At the supermarket checkout clerks always ask "Do you want your groceries bagged in paper or plastic?" The smart, environmentally aware consumers stop to think about their answers. They try to choose the material that will do the least damage to the environment and will do an adequate job holding the groceries.

There are a lot of environmental issues that smart consumers must consider. That is why this is a difficult question to answer. For example, consumers might ask whether the raw materials of paper and plastic bags are made from renewable or nonrenewable resources. Do the production processes of these two types of sacks cause pollution? Can the used sacks be reused or recycled? Are the sacks expensive to transport from the manufacturer to the grocery stores? (It takes more fuel to move heavy sacks than it does to move lightweight ones.) And what happens to the used sacks when they are thrown away?

Many paper and plastic bags are used only once and then tossed into the trash can. This is not the most environmentally responsible thing to do with an old sack, but it is very convenient. In this age of busy, mobile people, convenience often wins out over environmental good deeds.

When sacks are thrown away, they are usually taken to the landfill by city sanitation workers. The landfill is a place where trash is buried under layers of soil. Landfill space is at a premium. Everyone wants a landfill for burying trash, but no one wants that landfill near homes, schools, or jobs. Consequently, it is becoming difficult to find suitable places to build new landfills.

Most of the newest landfills are sealed so tightly that oxygen cannot diffuse into the buried material. Oxygen speeds decay and decomposition. Consequently, materials in landfills decay very slowly and remain the same shape and size for ten years or more.

If you are going to throw away sacks, perhaps you can help solve some of our landfill problems. In this lab, you will compare the mass and volume of paper and plastic sacks.

Prelab Questions

1. What are some questions that an environmentally conscious shopper might ask before choosing paper or plastic sacks?_____
   _____
   _____

2. Which would be least expensive to transport: soft drink bottles made of glass, or soft drink bottles made of plastic? _____ Why? _____
   _____
   _____

3. What do many people do with used sacks? _____
   What is the final resting place for these sacks?_____
   _____

4. Why do many people simply throw away materials that could be recycled?_____
   _____

5. Why is landfill space at a premium? _____
   _____

6. Why doesn't the trash buried in a landfill decompose? _____
   _____

Would You Prefer Paper or Plastic?

Objectives Compare the mass of paper and plastic sacks and the amount of space they occupy.

Materials
Plastic sack
Paper sack
Scissors
600-ml beaker
Triple beam balance

Procedure

1. Trim a large paper sack and a large plastic sack with scissors so that they are the same size (see Figure 1).

2. Cut the paper sack into small pieces.

3. Pack the pieces of paper sack in the beaker, pressing them down so that they occupy as little space as possible.

4. Record the number of millimeters of space occupied by the paper in the Data Table.

5. Remove all the paper from the beaker and place it on the triple beam balance. Record the mass of the paper in the Data Table.

6. Repeat steps 2-5 with the plastic sack.

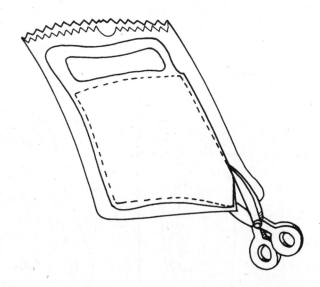

Figure 1. Lay one sack on top of the other. Trim the two sacks to be the same size.

Data Table. Mass and volume of paper and plastic sacks.

	Mass (in grams)	Volume (in milliliters)
Paper sack		
Plastic sack		

1. Which is heavier, the plastic or paper sack? _____ How much heavier? _____

2. Which takes up more space, the plastic or the paper sack? _____ How much more space? _____

3. If landfill space were the only consideration, would it be more environmentally correct to package your groceries in paper or plastic? _____ Why? _____

_____

4. If fuel conservation were the only consideration, would it be more environmentally correct to package your groceries in paper or plastic? _____ Why? _____

_____

5. One milliliter (ml) is equal to one cubic centimeter (cc). How much space did the paper sack occupy in cubic centimeters? _____ How much space did the plastic sack occupy in cubic centimeters? _____

You're a Big Sprout Now

Objectives

Students will determine how the temperature during germination affects the germination percentage of seeds.

Time Required

Day 1: 30 minutes
Day 2–14: 10 minutes per day

Teaching Strategies

Prior to the lab, have students read the Background Information and answer the Prelab Questions.

You will need access to a freezer or cooler and a refrigerator.

You may select any type of seeds to use in this lab activity. Radish and bean seeds germinate quickly, so these may be a wise choice for the activity.

Evaluation

Following is a suggested grading rubric:

Criteria	Points allowed	Points awarded
Prelab Questions correct	33.3	_____
Data Table complete	33.3	_____
Postlab Questions correct	33.3	_____
Total	100	_____

You're a Big Sprout Now

When farmers buy seeds to plant for their upcoming crop, they need to know what percentage of the seeds will germinate. Germination occurs when the embryo of the plant breaks through the seed coat and begins to grow (see Figure 1). The germination percentage is the number of seeds in every 100 that will sprout when exposed to the proper conditions. Some conditions that can affect the germination percentage are temperature, oxygen, water, and light. Most packages of seeds will have the germination percentage printed on them.

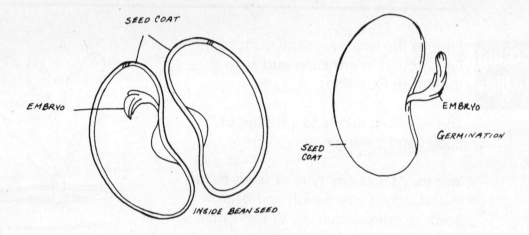

Figure 1.

Most of our main food crops are grown from seeds. Since seeds are very important in food production, there are specific laws to regulate the seed quality. Before seeds are packaged for people to purchase, the quality of the seeds is evaluated. The evaluation takes place in a seed-testing laboratory. Most states have their own seed-testing laboratory to monitor all seeds sold in that state. The seed-testing laboratory measures the purity of the seeds and the germination percentage. Seeds cannot be sold if they contain a large number of seeds from weeds mixed in with the pure seeds.

The seed germination percentage and date of testing are placed on the outside of most seed packages. A farmer must know the germination percentage of the seeds so he/she knows how many seeds to plant. If the germination percentage is 50%, the farmer will need to plant twice as many seeds to get the number of plants that he/she desires (see Figure 2).

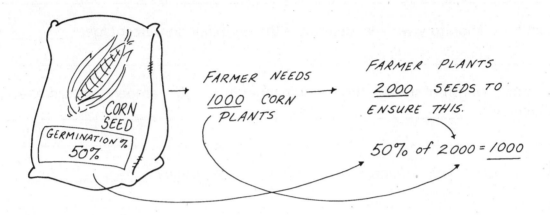

Figure 2.

Over time, germination percentage of seeds can decrease. The storage temperature of the seeds and the length of time the seeds are stored are factors in altering the germination percentage. Some seeds will not germinate after a year of storage, while others may continue to germinate for three or four years. The correct way to store seeds is in an airtight container at about 0 degrees C.

The germination percentage on the package of seeds may be higher than the percentage the farmer actually experiences. This is probably due to the special growing chambers the seed laboratory uses during testing. During these tests, the seeds are kept at a constant temperature. Obviously it is not possible to keep the soil temperature outside in fields and gardens constant.

Prelab Questions

1. What is *germination*? _____

2. What are some things that are tested for in the seed-testing laboratory? _____
   _____

3. Explain how laboratory workers determine the germination percentage. _____
   _____

4. Explain how length of storage time and changes in storage temperature can affect
   germination. _____
   _____
   _____

5. Why is the germination percentage important to the farmer? _____
   _____

You're a Big Sprout Now

Objectives
Students will determine how the temperature during germination affects the germination percentage of seeds.

Materials

Packages of seeds
3 petri dishes
Paper towels
Scissors
Water
Medicine dropper
Hand lens

Procedure

1. Label three petri dishes as A, B, and C.

2. Use scissors to cut three paper towels into circles that will fit into the bottom of a petri dish (see Figure 3).

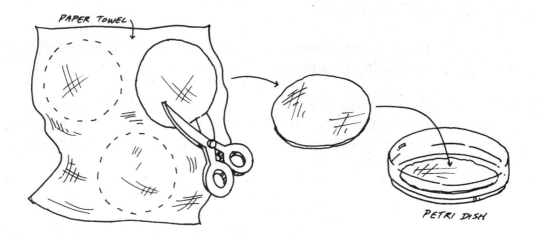

Figure 3. Cut three paper towels into three circles. Place each circle in the bottom of a separate petri dish.

3. Use the medicine dropper full of water to wet the paper towel circles in each petri dish. Saturate each paper towel thoroughly.

4. Place 25 seeds in dish A. Scatter the seeds so they do not touch one another in the dish. Cover the petri dish with the lid.

5. Scatter 25 seeds in dish B and 25 seeds in dish C. Cover both of these dishes with a lid (see Figure 4).

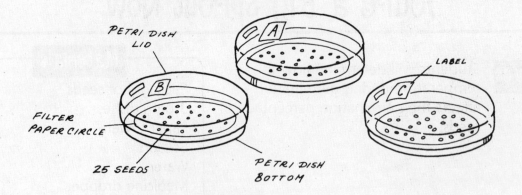

Figure 4. Twenty-five seeds in each petri dish

6. Place petri dish A in a place in your classroom where it will not be disturbed. These seeds will be allowed to germinate at room temperature.

7. Place petri dish B in a refrigerator.

8. Place petri dish C in a freezer.

9. Each day for the next two weeks, check each of these three petri dishes. If the paper towel in the petri dishes gets dry, add water to the dish.

10. Each day for the next two weeks, record the total number of seeds that have germinated in each dish. Place these figures in Data Table 1. You may want to use the magnifying glass to make certain you are actually seeing the emergence of the embryo from the seed.

Data Table 1. Number of seeds that germinate under various temperatures

Day	Total number of seeds that have germinated thus far Dish A	Total number of seeds that have germinated thus far Dish B	Total number of seeds that have germinated thus far Dish C
1			
2			
3			
4			
5			
6			
7			
8			
9			
10			

Postlab Questions

1. Multiply the total number of seeds that had germinated by the end of the second week by 4. This will give you the germination percentage. You multiply by 4 because you started with 25 seeds. If all seeds germinate, the germination percentage is 100. Show the germination percentage of all three petri dishes in the spaces below.

	Demonstration of your math	Final germination percentage
Dish A		
Dish B		
Dish C		

2. Look on the package of seeds that you used in this lab. How do the germination percentages on the package compare with your results?

_____

3. Does temperature appear to affect the rate of germination? _____
   Explain your answer._____

   _____

4. Name some other factors that can affect germination rate._____

   _____

Zeroing in on Food Preservatives

Objectives

Students will determine whether preservatives can prevent the growth of mold on white bread.

Time Required

30 minutes on Day 1
10 minutes a day for the next 10 school days

Teaching Strategies

Prior to the lab, have students read the Background Information and answer the Prelab Questions.

Divide the class into small groups of three or four.

Prior to the lab, take a trip to the grocery store and read the labels on several loaves of white bread. Select a loaf of white bread that lists preservatives and a loaf that does not list any preservatives. If you have trouble finding white bread without preservatives, try the health food stores. Some names of preservatives in bread include sodium bisulfite, sodium nitrate, and sorbic acid.

Take all the slices out of the sack of bread with preservatives and place them in a stack labeled A. Do the same for the sack of bread without preservatives but place them in a stack labeled B.

Prior to the lab, make overhead transparencies of "Grid Squares for the Lab." Use scissors to cut out the two grids on each page or have students do this prior to the lab. Each lab group will need one page of grid patterns.

Evaluation

Following is a suggested grading rubric:

Criteria	Points allowed	Points awarded
Prelab Questions correct	30	_____
Group on task during the lab	20	_____
Activity sheet completed correctly	20	_____
Postlab Questions correct	30	_____
Total	100	_____

Grid Squares for the Lab

Make some transparencies of this page so that each lab group has two grid patterns. Each grid pattern is composed of 25 squares.

Zeroing in on Food Preservatives

Almost all food we consume contains additives. An *additive* is a substance added in small amounts to something else to improve, strengthen, or alter it. A *food additive* is any substance that is intentionally added to food to improve its flavor, texture, appearance, nutritional value, or storage properties.

The use of additives to food is controlled by the government. In the United States the agency called the FDA (Food and Drug Administration) regulates the use of additives. All new food additives undergo extensive testing before they can be used in foods.

Certain additives are added to food to preserve the food and enhance its color and flavor. These chemicals are called *preservatives*. Many foods are produced far from where they are consumed. The only way to safely transport food long distances is to use preservatives. These substances help prevent spoilage and deterioration of food. Preservatives are a very popular way for retailers to extend the shelf life of foods in the stores.

Preservatives are usually chemicals that are used to prevent the growth of microorganisms that can ruin food. A preservative must be nontoxic and must not affect the flavor or color of the food.

Some common chemicals used as preservatives include sodium nitrate, sodium bisulfite, and sorbic acid. Natural substances like salt, vinegar, sugar, and spices are also preservatives, but since they are natural are not classified as additives.

Prelab Questions

1. What is a food *additive*? _____
_____

2. State some reasons for using food additives. _____
_____

3. What is a *preservative*? _____
_____

4. Explain why preservatives have become necessary in our society. _____
_____
_____

5. What is the role of the FDA in regulating food additives? _____
_____
_____

Zeroing in on Food Preservatives

Objectives Students will determine whether preservatives can prevent the growth of mold on white bread.

1 piece of bread from Stack A
1 piece of bread from Stack B
2 plastic bowls
Water
Medicine dropper
2 transparency grids
Black marker or tape

Procedure

1. Select a piece of white bread from Stack A.

2. Use a medicine dropper filled with water to completely wet the front and back of the bread slice.

3. Gently rub both sides of the wet bread slice on the floor or a table top.

4. Place the bread flat in one of the plastic bowls.

5. Label the plastic bowl as "A."

6. Lay the 25-square transparency grid on top of the piece of bread in the bowl.

7. Cover the bowl with clear plastic wrap.

8. Set the bowl and the bread slice in a warm place.

9. Repeat steps 1–9, but use bread from Stack B and label the bowl in which it is placed as "B."

10. Each day for the next ten school days, observe each slice of bread. Without removing the plastic wrap, count the number of grid squares in which you see mold growing. Mold will appear as a fuzzy growth on the bread.

Caution: Do not remove the plastic wrap from the bowls. Some people are very allergic to certain types of molds.

11. In Data Table 1, each day record the total number of squares that show mold growth.

12. At the end of Day 10, dispose of the containers in a special receptacle your teacher provides.

Data Table 1. Growth of mold on bread

Record of the number of squares infested with mold growth.

	Bread Slice A	Bread Slice B
Day 1		
Day 2		
Day 3		
Day 4		
Day 5		
Day 6		
Day 7		
Day 8		
Day 9		
Day 10		

Postlab Questions

1. Which bread contained the preservatives, A or B? _____ Defend your answer. _____

2. Do preservatives completely prevent the growth of mold? _____ Explain your answer._____

   _____

3. In which type of environment do you think mold grows best? (Circle one.)
   a. moist and cool   c. dry and cool
   b. moist and warm   d. dry and warm

   Explain your choice. _____

   _____

4. Do you think using preservatives in food is a wise thing to do? _____ Why or why not? _____

   _____

Answer Key

Bright Buttons

Prelab Questions   page 3
1. No. Some will not be as fit for survival as others. Some will die.
2. Answers will vary. A lizard that changes colors based on location in environment is one example.
3. Long wingspan. They would be better adapted to catch insects. Mottled brown. The white fawn would be easy for predators and/or hunters to see.

Postlab Questions   page 5
1. Check the Data Table to make certain students added their numbers properly.
2. Check to see that students performed their math correctly.
3. Check to see that students performed their math correctly.
4. Results should show that a higher percentage of bright-colored buttons were selected than dark-colored.

Cool and Comfortable

Prelab Questions   page 8
1. sweating
2. panting
3. As water evaporates from a surface, it uses up some of the heat on our body.
4. those that absorb and then release it

Postlab Questions   pages 10 and 11
1. Answers may vary. Cotton absorbs the greatest volume of water and silk the next greatest volume.
2. Cotton; it absorbs water and then releases it by evaporation, a cooling process.
3. Student answers may vary; to keep sheep dry when it rains.
4. the cup that contains the least volume of water
5. so that cloth size would not be a variable

Flipping Over the Elements

Prelab Questions   page 20
1. a display of known elements showing atomic number and atomic mass
2. in order of increasing atomic number
3. hydrogen
4. alkali metals
5. left, right
6. metalloids
7. 18; 7
8. lithium, antimony, and aluminum

Postlab Questions   page 21
1. sodium
2. As you move from top to bottom of a group, atomic number increases.
3. calcium
4. As you move from left to right of a period, atomic number increases.
5. Period 1 has 2, period 2 has 8, and period 4 has 18.

Freeze Warning

Prelab Questions   page 23
1. 100 degrees Celsius; 0 degrees Celsius
2. lowers the freezing point
3. When water freezes, it expands and can damage the radiator.
4. Water collects minerals and pollutants as it travels over the land.

Postlab Questions   page 25
1. cup A; cup C
2. adding salt
3. to compare water without additives to water into which we added things
4. It will allow the ice cream to freeze sooner than it would with only ice.

Hot Wired

Prelab Questions   page 28
1. atoms
2. two atoms of hydrogen and one of oxygen
3. slows them
4. expands the material

Postlab Questions   page 30
1. increased its length
2. shortened its length
3. Warm water causes the lid to expand so that it is not clamped so tightly around the jar.
4. In the summer, warm temperatures cause the wires to expand and sag.

Just Passing Through

Prelab Questions   page 33
1. the movement of molecules from a place of greater to lesser concentration
2. the membrane of the cell
3. A *solute* is the material that is dissolved in another substance, and the *solvent* is the material that does the dissolving of the solute.
4. solvent
5. the liquid and the solids dissolved in it

Postlab Questions   page 36
1. It dissolved the shell of the egg.
2. The egg looked larger and more dense.
3. The egg was shriveled and small.
4a. Water moved out of the egg.
4b. Water moved into the egg.
5. to determine whether or not the mass had changed. Changes in mass indicate diffusion has occurred.

I Sense Some Friction Here

Prelab Questions   page 39
1. *Force* is a push or pull that opposes motion.
2. As friction increases, motion slows unless more force is supplied.
3. On an icy surface there is not enough friction for your shoes to grab the surface of the earth.
4. oil, sand, or polish surfaces
5. Friction is not always the same. The amount of friction between two surfaces depends on the materials that make up the surfaces, the texture of the surfaces, and how tightly the surfaces are pushed together.

Postlab Questions   page 42
1. when the block was pulled over a regular surface
2. increase; requires more force to overcome the force of friction.
3. to reduce friction
4. There is less friction on ice and snow than on dirt.
5. On the regular surface; on the oiled surface

It's a Stick Up!

Prelab Questions   page 46
1. *Plastic* is a man-made substance created from raw materials such as crude oil and coal. Chemically, plastics are described as polymers.
2. A *polymer* is a long chain of repeating units; carbon.
3. the pop beads
4. They are flexible, or free to move around.

Postlab Questions   page 48
1. Answers will vary; water does not leak out after the plastic is skewered.
2. Answers will vary; the plastic that does not leak when skewered, the more flexible plastic, would be the best choice.
3. They are flexible.

Metric Matters
Prelab Questions   page 51
1. English
2. metric
3. meter
4. centimeter. Answers will vary.
5. millimeter. Answers will vary.
6. 8½ cm, 85 mm
7. kilometer; 1000
Postlab Questions   page 54
1. Answers may vary; students probably were most accurate on high power.
2. Low. On low power, the microscope lens takes in more space than it does on high power.
3. Answers may vary; some students may feel that they can accurately divide such small distances, while others may not.
4. Answers will vary.
5. a. 4 cm; b. 5.2 cm

Out in Space
Prelab Questions   page 57
1. solids, liquids, and gases
2. arrangement of particles in the phase
3. A liquid has a definite volume, a gas does not.
4. solid
5. Yes. Answers will vary.
Postlab Questions   page 60
1. A great deal of space is visible around the marbles. More was visible around the marbles than the sand.
2. More space was visible around the sand than the water. Virtually no space was visible around the water.
3. Answers will vary. You can expect from about 75 to 100 mL.
4. Answers will vary. You can expect from about 50 to 70 mL.
5. There will be from 1 to 10 mL difference.
6. Yes. Yes. The results of the lab verify this.

Penny Pushers
Prelab Questions   pages 62 and 63
1. The momentum of a moving object striking a stationary object will be transferred from the moving object to the stationary object. Momentum is not lost but transferred.
2. velocity and mass
3a. The parked car will travel a great distance forward due to the collision.
3b. The parked car will move forward but not as great a distance as if it had been hit by a truck.
4. The cue ball imparts its energy to the billiard ball and it moves forward.
5. Answers will vary. One example is a bat striking a baseball.
Postlab Questions   page 66
1. Answers may vary slightly, but "1 penny strikes 1 penny strongly" will be the probable choice.
2. yes. The stationary pennies moved a.greater distance when a strong collision occurred.
3. 1 penny striking 2 pennies strongly
4. 2 pennies striking 6 pennies softly
5. the speed and the number of pennies (size or force) used
6. Small cars are more apt to be crushed in collisions with larger cars.

Ticked Off
Prelab Questions   page 69
1. The particles of a solid are packed closer than those of a liquid. As the sound vibrates the particles of a solid, they bump against one another. This transfers the sound quickly.
2. The particles of a gas are much farther apart than the particles of a liquid. Particles of gases must travel farther to come into contact with other gas particles to transfer the vibration.
3. temperature
4. On foggy days, there is water vapor in the air. Sound travels more quickly through water than it does through air.

Postlab Questions   page 71
1. Answers will vary.
2. Answers will vary.
3. through a solid
4. Sound travels more quickly in a liquid than it does in a gas but more slowly than it does in a solid.

Would You Prefer Paper or Plastic?
Prelab Questions   page 74
1. Are the raw materials of paper and plastic bags renewable or nonrenewable resources? Do the production processes of these two types of sacks cause pollution? Can the used sack be reused or recycled? Are the sacks expensive to transport from the manufacturer to the grocery store? What happens to the used sacks when they are thrown away?
2. Soft drink bottles made of plastic; because they weigh less and therefore require less fuel to transport.
3. They throw them away. They are taken to the landfill.
4. It is more convenient to throw them away than it is to recycle them.
5. Most people do not want landfills built near their homes, jobs, or schools.
6. Because oxygen cannot reach the trash, and oxygen plays an important role in decomposition.
Postlab Questions   page 76
1. Paper is heavier; answers will vary, depending on the types of paper and plastic used.
2. paper. Answers will vary.
3. plastic; takes up less space in the landfill
4. plastic; not as heavy as paper and therefore cheaper to transport
5. Answers will vary.

You're a Big Sprout Now
Prelab Questions   page 80
1. *Germination* is the process of an embryo breaking through the seed coat and beginning growth.
2. purity and germination percentage
3. They test the number of seeds out of 100 that germinate in a controlled growing chamber at constant temperature.
4. Temperature changes and long storage times can decrease germination percentage.
5. Farmers need to know the germination percentage so they know how many seeds they need to plant to get the crop yield they require.
Postlab Questions   page 84
1. Results will vary, but students should find the germination percentage is higher at room temperature and in the refrigerator than in the freezer.
2. Answers will vary, but the percentage of all three petri dishes is probably lower than on the package.
3. Yes. Very cold temperatures can hinder germination.
4. Student answers will vary.

Zeroing in on Food Preservatives
Prelab Questions   page 88
1. An *additive* is a substance added intentionally to food to improve, strengthen, or alter the food.
2. Food additives can improve appearance, flavor, texture, nutritional value, and storage properties.
3. A *preservative* is a chemical used to prevent growth of microorganisms that can cause food to spoil.
4. We need preservatives because foods may be shipped long distances before they are consumed.
5. It tests to make certain additives are safe for human use.
Postlab Questions   page 90
1. Bread A had the preservatives. It had the least mold growth.
2. No. Preservatives only slow down but do not completely prevent mold growth.
3. Moist and warm. Those were the conditions to which the bread was exposed.
4. Student answers will vary.